Battle of Marston-Moor.

THE

BATTLE OF MARSTON-MOOR.

A LECTURE

DELIVERED

IN THE SCHOOL-ROOM, AT MARSTON,

BY

CAPT. THE HON. ROBT. NEVILLE LAWLEY.

The Naval & Military Press Ltd

Published by

The Naval & Military Press Ltd

Unit 5 Riverside, Brambleside
Bellbrook Industrial Estate
Uckfield, East Sussex
TN22 1QQ England

Tel: +44 (0)1825 749494

www.naval-military-press.com
www.nmarchive.com

Advertisement.

———

THE following Lecture was originally prepared for the information or amusement of those who reside in the immediate neighbourhood where the events narrated transpired. The Author had no thought of making the Lecture public ; and but for the urgent request of several friends who heard it delivered, it would have passed away with the occasion by which it was originated. The Lecturer did not feel at liberty to refuse compliance with the wishes of those in whose judgment he had the most perfect confidence :—hence the publication of the Lecture.

Every available source of information has been sought ; and the Author trusts that he has given a truthful representation of the events as they actually occurred. Of this, however, his readers must form their own opinion.

CONTENTS.

	PAGE.
Introduction	7
Disputes between the King and Parliament	8
The Star-Chamber—Taxes—Ship-money	9
The Rump-Parliament—Execution of Lord Strafford—Abolition of the Star-Chamber	9
Commencement of Hostilities	10
Battle of Edgehill	10
Character of the two Armies	11
Cromwell's Estimate of the Parliamentarian Army	11
Cromwell's Ironsides	13
Character of a Royalist, by a Royalist	15
Preliminary movements	18
Siege of York by the Parliamentarians	19
Prince Rupert marching to the relief of the City	20
Retreat of the Parliamentarians towards Marston-Moor ...	21
Letter from King Charles to Prince Rupert	23
Position of the two Armies	25
Plan of the Battle	27
Commencement of the Battle	34
Cromwell wounded...	36
Flight of the Right Wing of the Royalists	37
Flight of the Right Wing of the Parliamentarians	39
Rejoicing for the supposed victory of the Royalists	45
Cromwell to the Rescue	46
Final overthrow of the Royalists	48
The Field after the Battle...	50
Various Estimates of the Character of Cromwell	55
Clarendon—Carlyle...	55
Conclusion	56

Battle of Marston Moor.

1644.

BEFORE I enter into details upon the great Battle, fought on July 2nd, 1644, so near to the spot where we at present are ; I think it best to refer briefly to the lamentable events which had brought King Charles the first of England into civil war with his subjects and Parliament. King Charles came to the throne in the year of our Lord 1625, having been born in the first year of the seventeenth century, namely 1600,*—a date which I beg you will bear in mind.

The duty of the historian or lecturer is to be perfectly impartial ; and having had access to the very best contemporaneous and other accounts, I hope to "nothing extenuate, nor to set down aught in malice," in this Lecture. The seeds of animosity may be said now, (216 years after the event,) to have died out : but as long as England is a nation, the names of Cavalier and Roundhead, of King Charles and Oliver Cromwell, will be mentioned with thrilling interest. I may here notice, that the

* Cromwell was born in 1599.

Royalists, or King's party, in ridicule of the close cropped hair of the Puritans or Parliamentarians, gave the later the name of Roundheads in derision : while they, on their side, gave the Royalists the titles of Cavaliers or Malignants.

Please, however, to bear in mind, that the King himself was never here at Marston ; though the battle had a more disastrous effect on his fortunes, probably even than Naseby, which was fought one year later, or any other loss he sustained before his execution in 1649, in the 49th year of his age.

It was a great error in James 1st, father of Charles 1st, and one into which the latter also fell, to be occupied with abstract speculations upon kingly government, and not to see what passed under his eyes. Thus while James was writing books, and even composing Latin verses, he never perceived that his House of Commons was no longer that subservient body that it had been in all former years. Charles 1st seems to have been equally unaware of the fact, that from being the slave of former British Monarchs, Parliament was now able to be their ruler. The supplies which the Parliament had granted since his accession had been both scanty and grudgingly given ; and James 1st, his father, had left the treasury in such an exhausted state, that Charles, though frugal, soon found himself greatly embarrassed ; and even wanted money to defray the necessary expenses of the Government. He dissolved Parliament twice in the three first years of his reign, and even declared his determination to govern without one :

so that for eleven years, from 1629 to 1639, the King and the Star Chamber tried,—in an evil day for both,—to govern without Parliament at all.

Taxes were exacted with great severity, especially one called Ship-money for the Navy; but as it was considered illegal, the people became highly irritated. The ship-money was a tax laid upon all sea-ports, in consideration of their contributing a certain number of ships to the defence of the country. The King's favourite, Villiers, Duke of Buckingham, was accused of pocketing the proceeds. This, however, I do not believe to be true, as he certainly increased the number of ships, and the efficiency of the navy of that day. The Wits about Court called the tax, "a floating capital to keep him (Buckingham) above water." The King also tried to introduce Episcopacy into Scotland, with most indiscreet zeal ; and at last was obliged to summon another Parliament, (called the Long Parliament, and sometimes the Glorious or Rump Parliament) in 1640, in hopes that they would strengthen his power, and vote him money. The first acts of the Long Parliament were to enforce the execution of Thomas Wentworth, Lord Strafford, 12th May, 1641, and to abolish the Star Chamber. The first, a most unjust measure, which cost the King great pain to assent to; the last a most wise and salutary decree. Things went on from bad to worse, and the King was so weak as to concede to Parliament, in return for some supplies, the power to dissolve themselves without his royal order. Little did both *then* conceive that this Parliament would be dissolved thirteen years later, not by themselves, but by an English member of it, Oliver Cromwell, (one of those daring spirits who leave their footsteps on the sands of time,) with the aid of their own armed soldiers, April 20th, 1653.

In 1642, things came to a crisis, both parties drawing the sword, and throwing away the scabbard. The Royal Standard was unfurled at Nottingham, August 25th, 1642 ; and soon we hear of the King at York, receiving supplies from Holland, whither his Queen had fled.

The King had married, in 1625, Henrietta Maria, daughter of Henry 4th, one of the best Kings who ever sat on the throne of France. She was a rigid Papist, but pretty, clever, and attached to her husband. One of the Parliament Lords (Lord Paget) once arguing with her, said, that it (the Parliament) was a very Samson. "Aye," said she, and looking at him significantly, "I perceive wins battles like him, with the jawbone of an ass." She lived to see the restoration of her son, Charles 2nd, and died near Paris in 1669.

The first action was fought October 4th, at Edgehill, near Warwick, which was considered a drawn battle ; though the King's General, Robert Leslie, Lord Linsdey, was slain. In almost every shire, two hostile factions appeared against each other, and it is about this period I now allude to, viz. : 1643, that the incident related by Sandford about our village of Marston occurred. A traveller riding through the little hamlet, (for it could hardly be more then,) met a country man and asked him which he was for, King or Parliament,—a very

common question in those times. " Be they two
fallen out ? " was the simple reply.

At first, though the Parliament had much the
most money, the King had, during some months, a
decided superiority. His troops fought much better
than those of the Parliament. Both armies were
composed, it is true, of men who had never seen a
field of battle. Nevertheless, the difference was
great. The Parliamentary ranks were filled with
hirelings, whom want and idleness had induced to
enlist. Hampden's regiment was regarded as one
of the best ; but even this regiment was stigmatized
justly by Cromwell, as a mere rabble of tapsters
and men out of place. The royal army on the
other hand, consisted in great part of gentlemen,
high spirited, ardent, accustomed to consider dis-
honor more terrible than death, accustomed to
fencing, to the use of fire-arms, and to bold riding,
which has been well called the image of war. Such
gentlemen, mounted on their favourite horses, and
commanding little bands composed of their younger
brothers, game-keepers, huntsmen, and grooms,
were, from the very first day on which they took
the field, qualified to play their part with credit in
a skirmish. The steadiness, the prompt obedience,
the mechanical precision of movement, which are
characteristic of the regular soldier, these gallant
volunteers never attained. But they were, at first,
opposed to enemies as undisciplined as themselves,
and far less active, athletic, and daring. For a
time, therefore, the Cavaliers were successful in
almost every encounter.

The " Houses " too, as the Parliamentary side was generally called,—meaning, of course, the Lords and Commons,—had been unfortunate in the choice of their General, Robert Devereux, Lord Essex, who had, at the commencement of the war, as high a military reputation as any man in the country. But it soon appeared that he was unfit for the post of Commander-in-Chief. He had little energy, and no originality. The methodical tactics which he had learned in the foreign wars he had served in, did not save him from the disgrace of being surprised and baffled by such a Captain as Prince Rupert, who could claim no higher fame than that of an enterprising partisan.

Nor were the Officers much better, with the exception perhaps of Hampden, who was killed in a skirmish at Chalgrave, in 1643, and of those of the independent sect or party headed by OLIVER CROMWELL, or as he was called at the time I now describe, Colonel Cromwell. Bred in peaceful occupations, he had at more than forty years of age, accepted a commission in the Parliamentary army. No sooner had he become a soldier, than he discerned, with the keen glance of genius, what Essex and men like Essex, with all their experience, failed to perceive. He saw precisely where the strength of the Royalists lay, and by what means alone that strength could be overpowered. He saw that it was necessary to reconstruct the army of the Parliament. He saw, also, that there were abundant and excellent materials for the purpose ; materials less showy indeed, but more solid than those of which the gallant squadrons of the King were composed. It was necessary to look for recruits who were not mere mercenaries, for recruits of decent station and grave character, fearing God, and zealous for public liberty. With such men he filled his own regiment ; and while he subjected them to a discipline more rigid than had ever before been known in England, he ministered to their intellectual and moral nature stimulants of fearful potency.

The events of the year 1644 fully proved the superiority of his abilities. In the south, where Essex held the chief command, the Parliamentary forces underwent a succession of shameful disasters; but, as I shall proceed to show you, the superior talent of Cromwell and his Ironsides, procured a victory on Marston-Moor, which fully compensated for all that had been lost elsewhere. And here I must pause to assure you that, to this day, as some in this room can confirm, we soldiers of the Queen and established Church of England, still look back, as to a bright and shining light, to the successes of Cromwell, the great English Cavalry General. And never forget, that while he taught his men, as St. Paul says, to keep under their bodies (in other words, to practice the most rigid temperance and self-denial) he strove also to *elevate their souls.*

There is, however, an aspect of Puritanism in its social relations, which cannot be approached by any of us of the present day, without great self-distrust. The spell of a magician has been cast over this part of our subject ; and he must have extraordinary confidence in his own powers who can hope to remove completely the entrancing delusion. The

Cavalier and Roundhead of Sir Walter Scott's romances, will probably always remain too life-like and striking portraitures, not to be received by the majority of readers as faithful "reproductions" of the originals. The family portraits which hang round the galleries of our country houses are enlisted in aid of the delusion, if delusion it should be called. How many are there among those priestesses of our family portraits, the housekeepers of our great houses, who are conscientious enough, or think it consistent with their duty to the family, to own that an ancestor of their master fought against King Charles, instead of "suffering in the royal cause," as so many would seem to have done!*

The long flowing love-locks, the peaked beard and plumed hat of the "Cavalier," his rich and pictur-esque dress, and his gay dauntless bearing, have attracted irresistibly the sympathies of all, even to this day.

Most fortunate, also, were they in their painters of that day. The best picture of Cromwell, is by Sir Peter Lely, now in the Pitti Palace at Florence, of which I have a good copy at Hutton Hall. The expression is fine. Sir Anthony Van-dyke, who painted the original picture of Charles 1st, was undoubtedly the greatest portrait painter who ever lived. And when, as I said before, Sir Walter Scott, the great author of Waverley, threw life and reality into this pictorial fancy, and brought down the cavaliers from their dark old oak frames into the closest social sympathies of the present day,

* My own ancestor, Colonel Lawley, was killed in the Forest of Deane, on the side of the King, in 1643.

the illusion was rendered complete ; and every one would have been proud to welcome to his hearth and to his festive board the living man whose existence had been so entirely realized.

> " He has doff'd the silk doublet the breast-plate to bear,
> He has placed the steel cap o'er his long flowing hair ;
> From his belt to his stirrup his broadsword hangs down,—
> Heaven shield the brave gallant that fights for the crown.
> For the rights of fair England that broadsword he draws,
> Her King is his leader, her Church is his cause ;
> His watchword is honour, his pay is renown,—
> God strike with the gallant who fights for the crown."

Beautiful as these words are, however, God did not side with them, and contemporary royalist writers give us what may seem to be the reason. Dr. Edward Symmons, a minister of the Protestant Established Church of that day, and a royalist, says of his royal master and his troops ; "never had any good undertaking so many unworthy attendants, such horrid blasphemers and wicked wretches, as ours hath had ; we have those that seem to hate the name of religion, as much as the rebels hate loyalty." Of course the licentiousness of the majority of the cavaliers, is not to be taken as negativing the decency of the minority. But those individuals who attained to something like our modern ideas of a " gentleman," found themselves sadly out of place among the courtiers of King Charles. The Queen, moreover, imparted unhappily to the court of her husband, much of the empty heartlessness and unprincipled levity prevalent in the circles of the French Court, and indeed forestalled, in an approximate degree, the licentiousness of her son, Charles II.

Of course there were many differences on the subject of dress among the Puritans. Indeed, this has been a fertile cause of popular derision against them. But the puritan, or rather Parliamentary costume, though simple, and in comparison with the cavalier attire, plain and sombre, would be looked upon in the present day as offending on the side of foppery, rather than of quakerism. On the whole, it was extremely handsome and becoming. The military costume, therefore, would excite admiration in many instances, even in those accustomed to the uniforms of our household troops. The same may be said of the alleged close cropping of the hair, which gave them the name of Roundheads. This shortness of hair was only comparative to the exuberant locks of the Cavaliers, which would be considered extremely effeminate, and far more ridiculous than the puritan fashion, *now-a-days*.

Having now attempted to give you some idea of the position, costume, and discipline, of the two parties striving for the mastery in England, in the spring of 1644 ; it is necessary that I should lay before you the actual movements of the two armies, while I regret that I cannot offer for your inspection any of the weapons with which they did such execution. The sword, pistol, matchlock or carbine, and pike of those days, may be seen in the Tower of London. For artillery they had the culverin, or rude cannon of the day, drawn for the most part by oxen, to bring up which—the only incident still recorded here by the family of Acomb—taxed all the energies of the villagers. " Forward! Forward!" was Cromwell's constant cry, to the waggoners who drove these oxen, at the most critical time of the battle. They also had the demi-culverin and drake, each small and inconsiderable. But for the most part, it would appear as if the artillery of those days played a very unimportant part, to what we do now-a-days with the Armstrong gun. Gunpowder had been discovered some three hundred years, having been used, it is said, first at the battles of Poictiers and Cressy, in 1348. Though I believe the Chinese knew it still earlier. So imperfect, however, were the cannon of the fourteenth and fifteenth centuries, that they commonly burst at the third discharge. Nor will Cromwell's Ironsides bear comparison with Queen Victoria's ; the modern term of Ironsides being *now* applied to those huge floating batteries, the Warrior and Black Prince, which throw heavy shot weighing one hundred pounds at each discharge. Such shot, compared with the cannon-ball found near Wilstrop wood, now in my hand, would be as a gutter to a cataract, or a mountain to a mole hill. In a newspaper of the time, we read of Oliver Cromwell ; "This brave commander by reason of his resolution, and the gallantry of his charges, is called by the King's soldiers ' Ironsides.'" But the term was applied at last indiscriminately to him, or in the plural, to his troop, which beginning at about forty-two men, was ultimately brought into a double regiment of fourteen full troops, that is, as far as I can guess, about seven hundred sabres.

The execution that these noted troops, the Ironsides, did on our old hill-side yonder, is chiefly interesting as compared with modern statistics ; and, in this particular, the battle of Marston-Moor will bear comparison with any, even almost with those of the Crimea and Peninsula. The numbers at Albuera, in 1811, surpass it ; but there is none in the Crimea, bloody as it was, which, as the statistics are given, equals it ; while it surpasses the battle of Naseby next year, Worcester and Dunbar. Balaklava is the nearest approach to it in the Crimea ; but there, I regret to state, the English Light Cavalry were not successful.

To return, however, to the movements of the belligerents in 1664. In consequence of the inefficiency of the Earl of Essex, the Parliamentarians were commanded in the north by Edward Montague, Earl of Manchester, " a sweet meek man," as he is described, who permitted his Lieutenant, that is in Shakspear's sense, Lieut.-gen. Cromwell, to guide all the army at his pleasure. Cromwell had been occupied early in the year in conveying ammunition to Gloucester, and on the 6th of May, moving northward, took the town of Lincoln. The ancient citie of York was, however, a tougher nut for him to crack, being occupied, as old Drake the York Chronicler tells us, by many notable royalist leaders, who had every hope of being re-inforced soon by the arrival of the King's nephew, Prince Rupert. Accordingly, about the 3rd of June, after an attempt to storm the town near St. Mary's Church, which failed, the siege was converted into a blockade ; but the north-side of the town still remained open. You will understand, therefore, that at the end of June, 1644, the King's forces held the city of York, while the army of the Parliament encircled three sides of it.

The City had been besieged for nearly three months, and its provisions were getting very scarce, when on Friday, the 28th of June, news arrived of the advance from the south-west of Prince Rupert, with a numerous army. The leaders of the besieging armies remained for a day or two in their old positions, hoping to receive intelligence of the advance of auxiliary forces from the midland counties and Cheshire, under the Earl of Denbigh and Sir John Meldrum. Should these join them in sufficient time, they intended to continue the siege with a part of their forces, and with the rest give battle to the Prince. But letters now arrived from the Earl and Sir John that they could not be at Wakefield, until Wednesday night; and on Monday, the 1st of July, intelligence came that Rupert, with all his troops, was marching from Knaresborough towards the leaguer; whereupon, conceiving themselves unable to keep the siege and fight with him also, the Parliamentary Generals drew off all their forces from before the City; and on the same Monday morning, marched westward, and concentrated them on the Moor, which extended from the Ouse River southwards for upwards of six miles, between Poppleton, Redhouse, Monckton, and Long-Marston, and was called in its various parts, Ouse, Hessay, or Long-Marston Moor.

In the afternoon of that day, the Parliamentary soldiers were full of joy, expecting to have a battle with the enemy, being assured by their scouts that the Prince with all his forces would pass toward

York that way. But Rupert, having heard of their intention to force him to an engagement before his junction with Newcastle, disappointed them by a masterly move northwards ; and while a party of his horse faced them on the Moor, (having a bridge in the road to secure a retreat,) marched to Borough-bridge, and crossing over Thornton Bridge, placed the Ouse between himself and his opponents. The Earl of Manchester, foreseeing the possibility of some such movement, had ordered the construction of a bridge of boats at Poppleton, nearer to York, and had left a regiment of dragoons to guard it, intending to make use of it to pass his army over, in case of the Royalists marching towards the City by the north side of the river. But owing probably to the want of sufficient co-operation between the three Generals, Manchester's men were left un-supported, and without information of the Prince's near approach. Rupert, therefore, in his march along the northern bank of the Ouse, coming suddenly upon them, beat them away, and seized upon the bridge. The Generals were now unable to prevent his entrance into York, for the bridge they had built on the west side of the City was so weak, that they durst not venture to transport their armies upon it.

The Prince quartered his foot and ordnance thereabouts, and in the forest of Galtre, about five miles from York,—and not suffering them to go to that City, but keeping it in his power to enter thither with his whole army when it should be to his advantage, and to give and receive supplies as there should be cause. He then approached the

City himself, with two thousand horse ; and the Marquis of Newcastle immediately sent some persons to attend his Highness and invite him to enter York, there to consult together, and gain so much time as to open a port for the Marquis to march forth with the foot and cannon that were in the City, to join with the Prince's forces. " Upon this sad and unexpected disappointment to the Parliamentary soldiers, our hearts," says Mr. Ash, chaplain to the Earl of Manchester, " were filled with sorrow ; and the night drawing on, the foot-soldiers marched into the village of Long-Marston, about seven miles from York, where very few had the comfort of either convenient lodgings or food. The soldiers drank the wells dry, and then were obliged to make use of puddle-water ; most of the horse quartered on the Moor, and the Generals and Field-Officers met in earnest debate. They were divided in opinion what to do,—the English being for fighting, the Scots for retreating to gain (as they alleged) both time and place of more advantage, the Prince's army being now swollen to a considerable size."

The latter counsel prevailing, early the next morning (July 2nd) the armies were set in motion. A party of the royalist horse having again faced them awhile, and then wheeled back out of their sight, it was conjectured that Rupert was attempting to engage their attention, while with the main body he marched southwards, cutting off their provisions, and bursting into Lincolnshire and the associated counties. It was, therefore, resolved to march five or six miles in a southerly or south-west direction, towards Tadcaster,and those parts, whence they could protect or cover the forces from Cheshire and the midland counties, and also to pass the Ouse by a bridge of boats near Cawood, which would re-establish communications between the two sides of the river, stop the Prince from furnishing York with provisions out of the East or West Ridings, and so in time oblige him to fight. The Scots were in the van, followed by the English foot and all the artillery; while Sir Thomas Fairfax, Cromwell, and David Leslie brought up the rear with three thousand horse and dragoons. But they had again mistaken the intentions of Rupert, for nothing was further from his wishes than to avoid a general engagement.

The same morning, the Marquis of Newcastle went to wait upon the Prince, where after some conferences, he declared his mind to the Prince, desiring him not to attempt anything as yet upon the enemy, for he had received intelligence that there was some discontent between them, and that they were resolved to divide themselves, and so raise the siege without fighting; besides, he expected, within two days, Colonel Clavering with about three thousand men out of the north, and two thousand drawn out of several garrisons. But the Prince answered, that he had a letter from his Majesty, with a positive and absolute command to fight the enemy; which, in obedience, and according to his duty, he was bound to perform. The letter from the King was dated from Ticknell, and was as follows: " If York be lost, I shall esteem my crown little less, unless supported by your sudden march to me, and a miraculous conquest in the south, before the effects of the northern powers can be found here; but if you beat the rebel armies of both kingdoms which are before it, then, but otherwise not, I may possibly make a shift to spin out until you come to assist me: wherefore, I command and conjure you, by the duty and affection which I know you bear me, that you immediately march with all your forces to the relief of York; but if that be either lost, or have freed themselves from the besiegers, or that from want of powder you cannot undertake that work, you immediately march with your whole strength to Worcester, to assist me and my army; without which, or your having relieved York by beating the Scots, all the successes you can afterwards have, most infallibly will be useless to me."

Now, although there is a slight ambiguity in the letter, it is quite clear that the object aimed at was the relief of York; that beyond any engagement necessary to the accomplishment of that object no other was enjoined upon the Prince; nay, rather, there was the intimation of a desire that he should march southwards to join in the movements of the King himself. But the fiery Rupert caught eagerly at the mention of an engagement, and could not endure to have this anticipated honour dashed from his lips at the moment of possession. He therefore took care not to produce this letter; and its existence was evidently not credited by the Marquis, who replied, however, that he was ready and willing, for his part, to obey his Highness in all things, no otherwise than if his Majesty was

c

there in person himself; and although several of
his friends advised him not to engage in the battle,
because the command was taken from himself, he
replied that, happen what would, he would not
shun to fight, for he had no other ambition but to
live and die a loyal subject of his Majesty.

Battle was therefore resolved upon ; and after the
reconnoissance made by the body of horse before
mentioned, the Prince, perceiving that the Parliamentary forces were retreating from their positions, at about nine o'clock of the morning drew
over a great part of his troops by the bridge which
he had surprised the night before, and by a ford
near it, and marching after his enemy with about
five thousand horse and dragoons, (his foot following
more leisurely,) entered on the Moor near the
village of Long-Marston, and came close up to the
rear of their carriages.

The Scots were already within a mile of Tadcaster, and the Earl of Manchester's foot were two or
three miles beyond Marston, when there came a
very hot alarum from Sir Thomas Fairfax that they
must hasten back with all the speed they could
make ; for the Prince's army, horse and foot, were
upon their rear, and was likely to throw them into
some disorder ; that he hoped, however, by the
advantage of the ground he was on, to make it
good till they came back.   It would appear that
Fairfax and the cavalry had quitted the Moor, and
were on some fields of grain rising above it, and
separated from it by a ditch ; for we meet with no
account of a struggle for the possession of the

the Moor, which would hardly have been yielded by Fairfax without.

The Parliamentary foot instantly began to return, their horse in the meantime facing the Prince's foot, which were drawn up " so close to their noses," that they were unable to re-occupy any part of the Moor. " Hope of a battle," says Mr. Ash, " moved our soldiers to return merrily, which also administered comfort unto all who belonged unto the army," But before the foot could get back, the Prince's foot had come up in such numbers, as to secure themselves the entire possession of the Moor, so that the Parliament's Generals had abandoned to their opponents a most advantageous ground, and exposed themselves to all the risks of an unequal engagement while their army was in line of march. As the Parliamentary horse and foot came up, they were formed in battalia along the south side of the Moor, on the rising ground covered with fields of grain, called, from the village near them, " Marston fields." " Marston Moor," says a newspaper of the time, " is a few miles from Bramham Moor," where Mother Shipton prophesied a great battle would be fought ; " a very creditable approximation to true prophecy on the part of that ancient woman. The height of the corn, together with some showers of rain that then fell, proved no small inconvenience to the soldiers, as did the narrowness of the fields ; though these inconveniences were partly compensated by their having the advantage of sun and wind, and being on the higher ground. In the meantime, the Prince and the Marquis of Newcastle conferred

with several of their Officers about the drawing up
of their forces, and there were many disputes
concerning the advantages their enemies had : but
discovering that near a hill covered with rye, were
some clumps of trees, (one tree alone now remains,)
in front of the Moor, which was occupied by the
Parliament's cavalry, there was a place of great
advantage, where they would have both the sun
and wind of the latter, they advanced thither a
regiment of red-coats and a party of horse : but
they were repulsed, and the place covered by the
Parliament's wing. The morning and afternoon of
the 2nd of July were spent in drawing up the two
armies. A deep ditch and hedge ran along in front
of the King's forces, and were lined with four brigades of their musqueteers. Fifty thousand subjects
of one King stood face to face on Marston-Moor.

As the whole garrison of York were arrayed
here, except a small band left in the town under
Sir Thomas Glenham, being but eight miles from
the ancient city, the report of the cannon, and the
contradictory rumours, ever and anon arriving, must
have kept its inhabitants in restless agony. For
many a dear life was that day at deadly hazard ;
many a wife knew not if she were a widow ; and
many a venerable man who had grown old in the
service of that beautiful Minster, muttered with
trembling affection the petitions of the Liturgy,
which a near and mighty foe had sworn to efface,
even with blood. With what strange, what con-
flicting prayers was heaven besieged that day !
The numbers on each side were not far unequal, but never were two hosts speaking one

Plan of the Battle of Long-Marston Moor.

Wilstrop Wood.

Ordnance.

† † † †
(Reserve.)
† † † †

Irish Foot under Tillier and Bellasis.

RIGHT WING (5000 horse) under PRINCE RUPERT.

Horse Regiment under Lord Grandison.

Newark Horse, Irish Horse, Rupert's Life-Guards,
under Lord Byron.   under Sir R. Crane.

LEFT WING (Earl of MANCHESTER'S ARMY),
under LIEUT.-GEN. CROMWELL.

Scotch Dragoons, 5000 English Horse. 3 Brigades.
under
Colonel Frizeall.

| (Lieut.-Genl. | Eastern | (Maj.-Genl. |
| Cromwell.) | Counties' Ft. | Crawford.) |

Three Regiments of Scotch Horse,
under Genl. David Leslie.

Ordnance.

† † † † † †

Moor Lane.

ROYAL ARMY.

MARQUIS OF NEWCASTLE.

Ordnance.

† † † †
(Reserve.)
† † † †

Blue Regiment.

MAIN BATTLE (Foot), under GENERAL KING.

Rupert's Regt.   Porter's Div.   Newcastle's
(O'Neil.)   (Col. J. Russell.)   White-Coats.

Present Road to Tockwith from Marston.

PARLIAMENT'S ARMY.

MAIN BATTLE (Scotch Foot), under LIEUT.-GEN.
BAILIE.

Earl of Cassilis' Regt.   Earl of Lindsay's Regt.
Kelhead's Regt.   Lord Maitland's Regt.

Regiments of

Earl of   Earl of Loudon.   Earl of
Dunfermline.   Buccleugh.

Edinburgh.   Gen. Hamilton.   Lord Cowper.
A Brigade of Manchester's Foot.

(Earls of Manchester and Leven, and Lord Fairfax.)

(Reserve.)
Ordnance.
† † † †
EARL OF MANCHESTER.

LEFT WING (4000 Horse) under GEN. LD. GORING.

Lucas' Horse, King's Old Horse, under Hurry.

Musketeers.

Ordnance.

† † † † † †
(Reserve.)

RIGHT WING (LORD FAIRFAX'S ARMY).

Fairfax's   Fairfax's Horse (80 Troops.)
Foot.   under Sir Thomas Fairfax.
and Colonel Lambert.

Gap.   Scotch Lancers under
Cromwell's
Tree.   Earl of   Earl of   Lord
Dalhousie. Eglintoun. Balgonie.

2 Brigades of Scotch Foot.

(Reserve.)
Ordnance.
† † † † † †

Road to Wetherby.

Marston Village.

‖

Road to York

language of more dissimilar aspects. The Cavaliers flushed with recent victory, identifying their quarrel with their honour and their love, their loose locks escaping from beneath their plumed helmets ; glittering in all the martial pride which makes the battle-day so much like a pageant or a festival, and prancing forth with all the grace of gentle blood, as they would make a jest of death, while the spirit-rousing strains of the trumpets made their blood dance, and their steeds prick up their ears. The Roundheads, arranged in thick dark masses, their steel caps and high crown hats drawn close over their brows, looking determination, expressing, with furrowed foreheads and hard-closed lips, the inly-working rage which was blown up to furnace-heat by the extempore effusions of their preachers, and which found vent in the terrible denunciations of the Hebrew psalms and prophecies. The arms of each party were adapted to the nature of their courage ; the swords, spikes and pistols of the Royalists, light and bright, were suited for swift onset and ready use ; while the pondrous basket-hilted blades, long halberts, and heavy fire-arms of the Parliamentarians were equally adapted to resist a sharp attack, and to do execution upon a broken enemy.

The Royalists regarded their adversaries with that scorn which the gay and high-born always feel or affect for the precise and sour-mannered ; the soldiers of the covenant looked on their enemies as the enemies of Israel, and considered themselves as the elect and chosen people, a creed which extinguished fear and remorse together. It would be

hard to say whether there were more praying on
one side, or swearing on the other ; or which, to a
truly Christian ear, had been the most offensive.
Yet both esteemed themselves the champions of
the Church. There was bravery and virtue in
both ; but with this advantage on the Parliamentary side, that while the aristocratic honour of the
Royalists could only inspire a certain number of
gentlemen, and separated the patrician from the
plebeian soldier, the religious zeal of the Puritans
bound officer and man, general and private, together in a fierce and resolute sympathy, and made
equality itself an argument for subordination. The
Captain prayed at the head of his company, and
the General's oration was a sermon.

The royal army spread themselves along the Moor
in a great many small bodies, extending, as it was
calculated, for about two miles in length ; Rupert's
forces forming on the right, and the Marquis of
Newcastle's on the left. Their left wing, which
" rested on some broken ground covered with gorse,"
consisted of four thousand horse (with reserves)
commanded by George Lord Goring, general of
Newcastle's cavalry, and under him Lieut,-general
Sir Charles Lucas and Sir John Hurry, who had
already changed sides during the war. The right
was under the command of Rupert himself, and
consisted of about five thousand picked horse, drawn
up in twelve divisions, containing a hundred troops.
They were made up by the Newark horse and Irish
catholics, under Lord Byron, and Rupert's own
brigade of cavalry, backed by a horse regiment,
under the Lord Grandison ; a body of Irish foot led

by Major-general Tillier and Colonel Bellasis, acted
as a reserve behind this wing. The centre composed
of foot, were under the command of Lieut.-general
James King, a Scotch commander of very doubtful
military reputation, and who had been lately raised
by Charles to the title of Lord Eythyn or Itham.
The right of this body was composed of Rupert's
regiment of foot under O'Neil ; the left of the Marquis of Newcastle's gallant brigade of his own ten-
antry, styled " Whitecoats." Between these was
a division of infantry, commanded by Major-general
George Foster. The reserves were a body of foot
called the blue regiment. The army was supported
by twenty-five pieces of artillery ranged along the
whole line, and particularly on either wing.

On the Parliament's side, the Earl of Leven and
the other two generals hastened from place to place
to put their forces in battle array, their pioneers
endeavouring to get ground to extend the wings of
the army to a convenient distance, which it was very
difficult to attain. The right wing was placed just
by the village of Long-Marston, the village being on
their right hand, and the army fronting towards the
east. The utmost point of their left wing extended
to Tockwith, (a village to the northwest of
Marston ;) so that the whole army fronted Long-
Marston Moor from Marston to Tockwith, a distance
of a mile-and-a-half. The wings of the King's forces,
drawn up just under them, extended rather further
on both sides than the line of their opponents ; but
the flanks of the latter were protected by the hedges,
and a party of Scotch dragoons under Colonel
Frizeall. The Parliament's troops, when at length

drawn up, spread themselves along the rising ground in the following order. Close to the village of Long-Marston lay their right, consisting of Lord Fairfax's army. The extreme point on the right was composed of some five thousand cavalry, drawn up in eighty troops, commanded in chief by Sir Thomas Fairfax. This comprised his English horse under Colonel Lambert, backed by three regiments of Scotch horse under the Earls of Dalhousie, Eglinton, and the Lord Balgonie, (Leven's eldest son.) Next came Fairfax's English foot—the men of Yorkshire and the northern counties, with two brigades of Scotch foot as a reserve. The middle centre was occupied by the Earl of Leven's Scotch foot, under his Lieut,-general John Baillie ; the van being composed of the Earl of Lindsay and Lord Maitland's regiments on the right, and those of the Earl Cassilis and Douglas of Kelhead on the left. In the rear of these was a reserve, consisting of the regiments of the Earls of Dunfermline, London, and Buccleugh ; the Lord Cooper and Sir Alexander Hamilton, (general of the artillery, and then better known by the name of ' Deare Sandie,') the Edinburgh regiment, and a brigade of the Earl of Manchester's English foot. In the centre was drawn up the Earl of Manchester's army from the associated counties, under the general command of Lieut.-general Cromwell, consisting of three brigades of foot, commanded severally by Colonels Montagu, Russel, and Pickering, and under the general command of Major-general Crawford ; and to the left of them, about five thousand horse, drawn up in five bodies and seventy troops, under Cromwell's immediate command, comprehending Manchester's cavalry, backed by three troops of Scotch horse, under Major-general David Leslie. Beyond them, on the extreme left, and close upon Tockwith, were Colonel Frizeall and the dragoons, with whom was Colonel Skeldon Crawford.

By about two o'clock of the afternoon, the two armies were drawn up in complete battle array, the royalists having been engaged till then in bringing over a part of their foot from the other side of the Ouse. The numbers on both sides were nearly equal, the Prince having some 23,000 or 24,000 men, the Parliamentarians somewhat more. The great ordnance then began to play, but (as usual in that century) with but small effect. About five o'clock, there was general silence, each expecting who should begin the charge, as the ditch and hedge bank must be crossed by the Roundheads, if they would attack the Cavaliers on the moor ; or by the latter, if they would charge their opponents in the great rye-field and closes ; so that a great disadvantage would result to those that began the charge, seeing the ditch must somewhat disturb their order, and the others would be ready on good ground and in good order to charge them before they could recover it. It may have been during this interval of inaction that Prince Rupert himelf examined a prisoner as to who were the leaders of the opposing army. The man answered ; General Leven, my Lord Fairfax, and Sir Thomas Fairfax. " Is Cromwell there ? " exclaimed the Prince, interrupting him, and being answered that he was; "Will they fight?" said he, "if they will, they shall have fighting enough!" The soldier was then relased, and returning to his own army, told the generals what had passed, and Cromwell that the Prince had asked for him in particular, and said they should have fighting enough.. "And," exclaimed Cromwell, "if it please God, so he shall."

But it seemed as if the wishes of neither of their commanders were on this occasion to be gratified; for seven o'clock arrived, and the armies still remained gazing silently on each other. "And surely," says Scout Master Watson, "had two such armies, drawn up so close to one another, being, on both wings, within musket-shot, departed without fighting, I think it would have been as great a wonder as hath been seen in England!" That this would be the case, at least for that night, was the opinion of both sides; and on the Marquis of Newcastle asking the Prince on what service he would be pleased to command him, the latter answered, that he would begin no action upon the enemy till early the next morning, desiring the Marquis to repose himself till then; which he did, and went to rest in his own coach that was close by in the field, until the time appointed.

But his rest was destined to be short; for Prince Rupert having erected a battery on the Moor, opposite to the left wing of the Parliament's forces, Cromwell ordered two field-pieces to be brought forward from the hill on which they had been planted, appointing two regiments of foot to guard them. These, marching for that purpose, were attacked by the musqueteers of the Royalists right wing, who fired quickly upon them from the ditch. This, in a moment, brought on a general engagement, at about half-past seven in the evening. The Royalist signal was to be without bands and scarfs, and their word, " God and the King ; " their opponents' signal was a white paper or handkerchief in their hats, and their word, " God with us." The sign being given, the left of the Roundheads marched down to charge, Cromwell with his horse coming off the coney-warren by Bilton bream. " And now you might have seen the bravest sight in the world, for they moved down the hill like so many thick clouds." They were divided into brigades of foot of 800, 1000, 1200, and 1500 men each : and each brigade of horse consisting of three or four regiments. " We came down the hill," says Watson, who was with Cromwell's horse, " in the bravest order, and with the greatest resolution that was ever seen." The Earl of Manchester's foot began the charge against some of the bravest of Newcastle and Rupert's foot, Colonel Frizeall and his dragoons acting their parts admirably, and driving before them the Musqueteers in the ditch and the Royalists daunted and amazed at this sudden attack, after a short firing on both sides, retreated from the ditch, leaving four " drakes " behind them. Lord Byron, unable at this sight to restrain himself until his opponents had crossed, dashed impetuosly over the ditch, throwing his men into considerable disorder, and being immediately driven back.

The Royalists never seem to have learnt, till too late, that a pitched battle is not a hunting-day.* Advancing to the charge with the same light hearts, and pursuing their game with as little consideration as if the business were a chase, they were no match for serious fighters like Oliver and Fairfax. "In a moment," continues Watson, "we passed the ditch on to the Moor upon equal terms with the enemy, our men going in a running march. Our front divisions of horse charged their front, Cromwell's own division of three hundred horse, in which himself was in person, charging the first division of Prince Rupert's in which himself was in person, and in which were all their gallant men, they being resolved, if they could scatter Cromwell, all were their own." "The rest of our horse," he continues, "backed by Leslie's three troops, charged other divisions of theirs, and with such admirable valour, as to astonish all the old soldiers of the army. Cromwell's own division had a hard struggle, for they were charged by Rupert's men both in front and flank." The troopers on both sides first discharged their pistols, then flinging them at each others heads, they fell to it with their swords. ˙A shot grazed the neck of Cromwell, and caused some fear in his men, lest he was severely hurt. "For awhile they stood at the sword's point, hacking one another, and the result was doubtful; but at last Cromwell broke through, scattering them before him like a little dust." At

* In the old letters bearing that date, it is said that the Yorkshire Gentlemen hunted and killed a stag in the neighbourhood that very day!

the same instant, the rest of the horse of that wing had wholly broken all Prince Rupert's horse on their right wing, and they fly along by Wilstrop Wood-side as fast and as thick as could be. Cromwell and Leslie sending a party in pursuit, proceeded onward with the main bodies. "Manchester's foot," says Watson, "charging by our side, dispersing the enemy's foot, almost as fast as they charged them, still going by our side, cutting them down ; so that we carried the whole field with us, thinking the victory ours, and nothing to be done but to kill and make prisoners." In this struggle, the brigades of Colonels Montagu, Russell, and Pickering particularly distinguished themselves, "standing when charged like a wall of brass, and and letting fly small shot like hail," upon the Royalists ; and yet, as an old account assures us, not a man of their brigades was slain.

Meanwhile, the Marquis of Newcastle had not been long in his coach when he heard "a great noise and thunder of shooting," which gave him notice of the armies being engaged. Whereupon he immediately put on his armour, and was no sooner got on horseback but he beheld a dismal sight,—all the horse and foot of the King's right wing in full flight ; and although he made them stand once, yet they immediately betook themselves to their heels again, and killed even those of their own party that endeavoured to stop them.

But in every other part of the field the result was very different. Between the right wing of the Parliament and the Royalists "there was no passage across the ditch, except a narrow lane, where

they could not march above three or four in front;
on one side of the lane was a ditch, and on the
other a hedge, both of which were lined with
Royalist musqueteers." This lane, called the
" Moor-lane," still remains, branching off at right-
angles from the road from Marston to Tockwith,
and leading directly to the Moor. It passes
through fields of grain, and is still separated from
them by a hedge on each side. About half-way
down, you reach a gate ; and either here, or still
further down the lane, turning to the left, where
four lanes meet, and so emerging on a large field
still called, par excellence, " Marston Moor," Fairfax's troops entered on the Moor. There are
traces of ditches and old hedges in both spots ;
and while the latter corresponds best to the account in other respects, it seems much too far from
Marston, and too much to the left. Some half
century ago a dyke, near to the latter spot, called
" the White Syke drain," was cleared out and
deepened, and then a large number of old-fashioned
horses' shoes, cannon-balls, the blade of a sword
lying by the side of its hilt, and other relics of the
struggle, were dug up, and distributed amongst the
inhabitants. The Moor-lane itself got a bad name
in consequence of the bloodshed of which it was
the scene ; and I am told that, in the last century,
the rustics were afraid of venturing there by night,
as they fancied they encountered headless horse-
men.

Before Sir Thomas Fairfax's horse could get to
the enemy, they were thrown into great disorder
by the furze and other bushes they had to pass

over. Fairfax, however, drew up a body of four thousand horse, and charged the left wing of the Royalists, whose intervals of horse were lined with musqueteers, who did great execution with their shot. Sir Thomas charged with great gallantry; and for a long time the struggle was most severe, the Royalists keeping themselves in a body, and receiving his troops by threes and fours as they marched out of the lane. In the heat of the fight, Fairfax was heard calling out to his officers and soldiers to be "merciful to the common men, for they, alas! were seduced, and knew not what they did; but to spare neither Irish nor buff-coats and feathers, for they were the instrument of their miseries!" At last, Sir Thomas broke through that part of the Royalist wing which he had charged, and routing them, pursued them a good way towards York. He himself hasted back to lead on the rest of his men; but before he could reach the scene of action, the battle was lost on that side, for the part of the Royalist wing which remained on the field, perceiving the disorder of Fairfax's men, charged them with great spirit, and crying out, "They run in the rear!" the newly-levied regiments, which were in the van, wheeled about, and fled back on their own foot in inextricable confusion, hotly pursued by the Royalists. "I must ever remember with thankfulness," says Sir Thomas Fairfax, "the goodness of God to me this day; for, on returning back, I got in among the enemy, who stood up and down the field in several bodies of horse. So, taking the signal out of my hat, I passed through them for one of their

D

commanders, and got to my Lord of Manchester's horse in the other wing, only with a cut in my cheek, which was given me in the first charge, and a shot which my horse received. In this charge many of my officers and soldiers were hurt and slain, as many as in the whole army besides, and there was scarce any officer but received a hurt. Colonel Lambert, who should have seconded me, but could not get up to me, charged in another place, and had his horse killed under him. Major Fairfax (the Major of his regiment) received at least thirty wounds, of which he afterwards died at York; and my brother (Sir Charles Fairfax) being deserted of his men, was sore wounded, of which, in three or four days he died, in the twenty-third year of his age, and was buried at Marston."

The two squadrons of Balgonie's regiment, being divided each from the other, one of them being lancers, charged a regiment of the Royalist foot, and cutting a passage through them, made their way with what remained of their soldiers to the Parliament's left wing; the other squadron in the end managed to rally and joined them also. The Earl of Eglington's regiment for some time maintained their ground (most of the Royalist horse going in pursuit of the rest of the wing) but with great loss, including the Earl's son, who was mortally wounded; until at length they also were swept away in the general flight of the Parliament's right wing.

Nor had Fairfax, on the Parliamentary right, better success; for, after beating off the Royalists from the hedge before them, and driving them from their cannon (two drakes and a demi-culverin,) they were met by the Marquis of Newcastle's gallant regiment of Whitecoats, who furiously assaulted them, and drove them back in complete disorder. At this moment, the broken troops of Sir Thomas Fairfax were hurled back upon them by the victorious Royalist cavalry, breaking them wholly, and trampling most of them and the Scotch reserve under foot. Part of the Royalist horse charged through the broken masses to the top of the hill, where the carriages and ordnance of the Parliament were placed ; and the waggoners and carters, terrified at their approach, quitting their charge in hasty retreat, they fell to plundering, without regard to the fate of the day, which they considered to be already decided. General Goring and Sir Charles Lucas, with the rest of the royal horse, having dispersed the right wing of their opponents, assaulted the main body of Scotch foot . upon their flank.

The struggle here had been very fierce, and until then without any result. On the Earl of Leven giving the signal to advance, the middle centre was led on by Hamilton and Baillie, the reserve being committed to the trust of Major-general Lumsdaine. The van assaulted the musqueteers in the ditch with great spirit, and drove them from their ground ; and Manchester's foot, under Laurence Crawford, having, in their victorious advance on the left, over-winged the Royalist foot in the centre, set upon their flank, and thus gave occasion to the Scotch foot to cross the ditch. "The Scotch gave fire so expertly, that it seemed as if the element itself had been on fire.*

It was while the struggle was undecided in this quarter, and the confusion was at its height, that the Marquis of Newcastle appeared on the field, and, accompanied by his brother, Sir Charles Cavendish, and three others, hastened to see in what state his own regiment of Whitecoats was. On his way, he met with a troop of gentlemen volunteers who formerly had chosen him for their captain, to whom he called out, "Gentlemen, you have done me the honour to choose me your captain, and now is the fittest time that I may do you service ; wherefore, if you will follow me, I shall lead you on the best I can, and show you the way to your own honour." They, being as glad of this proffer as he of their readiness, went on with the greatest courage ; and passing through two bodies of foot, (engaged with each other at less than forty yards distance,) received not the least hurt, as the Marquis assures us, although these bodies fired quickly upon each other. They then marched towards a Scotch regiment of foot, which they charged and routed ; in which encounter, we are assured, the Marquis killed three men with his page's half-leaden sword, having no other left him. After dashing through this regiment of foot, the whole troop was brought to a stand by a resolute pikeman, who though charged by Newcastle two or three times, stood his ground, till overpowered by numbers, he was cut down and despatched. In

* Numbers of them lie buried in Bilton Church Yard.

all these encounters the Marquis received no hurt, though several of his men fell around him.

The left wing of the Royalists now came thundering on the flank of the Scotch centre, while Newcastle and King pressed upon their van. They resisted bravely, and having inter-lined their musqueteers with pikemen, twice made their enemies give ground. Baillie and Lumsdaine, perceiving the weight of the battle to lie sore on the Earl of Lindsay and Lord Maitland's regiments on the right van, against which Newcastle's victorious Whitecoats and Goring's victorious horse directed their utmost efforts, sent up a reserve for their assistance; but the royalist horse charging a third time, the Scotch broke in every direction, Lumsdaine, the Earl of Lindsay, and Lieut-colonel Pitscottie (the Colonel of Maitland's regiment) alone standing their ground with a few men of their regiments. The Earl of Leven in vain hastened from one part of the line to the other, endeavouring by words and blows to keep the soldiers in the field, exclaim-ing,—" Though you run from your enemies, yet leave not your general ; though you fly from them, yet forsake not me ! "

The Earl of Manchester, who this day exercised rather a general control as field-marshal than any particular command, with great exertion rallied five hundred of the fugitives, and brought them back to the battle. But these efforts to turn the fate of the day in this quarter were fruitless, and at length the three generals of the Parliament were compelled to seek safety in flight. Leven himself, conceiving the battle utterly lost,—in which he was confirmed by the opinion of others then on the place near him, seeing they were fleeing upon all hands towards Tadcaster and Cawood,—was persuaded by his attendants to retire, and wait his better fortune. He did so, and never drew bridle till he came to Leeds, having ridden all that night with a cloak of drapde-berrie about him, belonging to the gentleman from whom we derive the information, then in his retinue, with many other Officers of good quality. Manchester and Lord Fairfax, carried away in the flight, soon returned to the field, but the centre and right wing of their army were utterly broken.

" It was a sad sight," exclaims Mr. Ash, ." to behold many thousands posting away, amazed with panic fears ! " Many fled without striking a blow, and multitudes of people that were spectators ran away in such fear as daunted the soldiers still more, some of the horse never looking back till they got as far as Lincoln, some others towards Hull, and others to Halifax and Wakefield, pursued by the enemy's horse for nearly two miles from the field. Wherever they came, the fugitives carried the news of the utter rout of the Parliament's army ; and the intelligence spreading through Yorkshire, reached the ears of the Royalist Governor of Tickhill Castle, (about five miles south of Doncaster,) by whom it was transmitted to Newark, and from thence to Oxford, by an express messenger ; and on the Friday there were ringing of bells and

bonfires at Oxford and Newark, for the great
victory God had given Prince Rupert over the
forces of three Generals before York; that he
had taken one of them, slain another, and utterly
routed their armies, and taken all their ordnance
and ammunition. At Banbury and other places
there were like rejoicings; and the news going
westward, gladdened the heart of King Charles
in a campaign he was undertaking, and caused
violent disputes between the governor of Exeter
(Sir John Berkeley,) and the Earl of Essex, as
to its accuracy.

The extraordinary appearance of the battle-field,
at this time, is graphically described by a Mr.
Trevor, in a letter to the Marquis of Ormonde,
both royalists. " I could not (he says,) meet the
Prince until after the battle was joined ; and in the
fire, smoke, and confusion of the day, I knew not
for my soul whither to incline. The runaways on
both sides were so many, so breathless, so speech-
less, so full of fears, that I should not have taken
them for men but by their motion, which still
served them very well, not a man of them being
able to give me the least hope where the Prince was
to be found, both armies being mingled, both
horse and foot, no side keeping their own posts.
In this terrible distraction did I scour the country ;
here meeting with a shoal of Scots crying out,
' wae's us! we're a'undone !' and so full of lamen-
tation and mourning, as if their day of doom had
overtaken them, and from which they knew not
whither to fly. And anon I met with a ragged
troop, reduced to four and the cornet ; bye and bye,

a little foot-officer, without a hat, band, or indeed
anything but feet, and so much tongue as would
serve to inquire the way to the next garrisons,
which, to say truth, were filled with stragglers on
both sides within a few hours, though they lay
distant from the place of fighting twenty or thirty
miles."

It was at this crisis of the fight that the left of
the Parliament's forces, under Cromwell, having
cleared the field on their side, and taken all the
Prince's artillery and ammunition, came sweeping
round to the part of the Moor formerly occupied
by the royalist left, hoping that their own right had
done as good service as themselves. But the
remnant under Sir Thomas Fairfax and Lambert,
having informed them of the fate of the battle in
the other quarters; neither wearied by their former
hot service, nor discouraged by the sight of that
strength which the royalists had still unshaken and
entire, they, that is Cromwell's division, came on
in excellent order to a second charge. " And here
(says Watson) came the business of the day to be
disputed; for the enemy seeing us to come in such
a gallant posture to charge them, left all thoughts
of pursuit, and began to think that they must
fight again for that victory which they thought had
been already got; they marching down the hill upon
us from our carriages, so that they fought upon the
same ground, with the same front that our right
wing had before stood to receive their charge on,
and we stood upon the same ground, with the same
front which they had when they began the battle.
Our three brigades of foot of the Earl of Man-

chester being on our right hand, on we went, with great resolution, charging them home, one while their horse, and then again their foot, and our foot and horse seconding each other with such valour, with such sound charges, that away they fled, not being able to endure the sight of us, so that it was hard to say which did the better, our horse or foot. Major-general Leslie seeing us thus pluck a victory out of the enemy's hands, could not too much commend us, and professed Europe had no better soldiers ! "

Cromwell and Leslie carried everything before them, till they came to the Marquis of Newcastle's foot battalion of Whitecoats, who first peppering them soundly with their shot when they came to charge, stoutly drove them back with their pikes. Here the Parliament's horse of that wing received their greatest loss, and a stop for some time was put to their hoped-for victory ; until at length the Scotch regiment of dragoons, commanded by Colonel Frizeall, with two others, being brought to bear upon their flank, and their ammunition being spent, an opening was made in their line, and thirty being made prisoners, the rest refusing quarter, every man of them fell in the same order and rank in which he had fought. "The Whitecoats (Royalist volunteers) showed such extraordinary valour and courage in the action, that they were killed in rank and file." Cromwell and Leslie then charged a brigade of Greencoats, and cutting down a great number, put the rest to the rout ; and charging the remainder of the Royal horse with like success (Sir Charles Lucas being unhorsed and taken prisoner,)

by about nine o'clock had cleared the field of all
enemies, recovered their own ordnance and carriages, and taken all those of the Royalists. "We
followed the chase of them," says Watson, "to
within a mile of York, cutting them down, so that
their dead bodies lay three miles in length;" "the
moon with her light, according to others, helping
something the darkness of the season."

An opening in a hedge, separating some fields
which lie between Marston-village and the rye-hill,
is still pointed out as indicating the spot where the
vengeful sword of Cromwell's soldiers overtook the
flying Royalists. From this tradition, it bears the
name of Cromwell's Gap; and the story runs, that
the grass would not grow on the ground stained
with so much loyal blood; others say that it is
where Cromwell's artillery was dragged; but certain
it is that to this day no thorn will grow there.

The Marquis of Newcastle was the last in the
field; and seeing that all was lost, and that every
one of the King's party made his escape in the best
manner he could, he being moreover inquired after
by several of his friends, who had all a great love
and respect for him, escaped towards York late at
night, accompanied only by his brother and one or
two servants; and coming near the City in front of
which General King had drawn up such of the
fugitives who had reached the shelter of its walls,
met the General and Prince Rupert, the latter of
whom had with great difficulty escaped from the
Moor, having lost his horse and hat, and being
obliged (as it is said) to conceal himself for a short
time in a bean field. Rupert eargerly inquired how

the business went? to whom the Marquis answered, "that all was lost and gone on their side." On this, Rupert is said to have exclaimed, "I am sure my men fought well, and know no reason of our rout but this, because the Devil did help his servants!"

What followed shall be given in the words of Rupert's Chaplain. "Says General King, 'What will you do?' Says Lord Newcastle, 'I go into Holland,' looking upon all as lost. The Prince would have him endeavour to recruit his forces; 'No,' says he, 'I will not endure the laughter of the court;' and King said he would go with him.

Meanwhile, the Parliament's soldiers were availing themselves of the fruits of their victory. "The Prince of 'Plunderland,'" says an old account, (Rupert had been created Duke of Cumberland, January 24th, 1644,) "he that had by day-light plundered others, had his rich sumpter plundered by moon-light; for till twelve at night our soldiers had the slaughter of the enemy in woods and lanes and fields. This hamper or sumpter was found in the wood, with a guard to defend it. Our soldiers do not love to tell what *was in it*; only they say some papers with C. R., that he should fight, whatever came of it.

Manchester's army, we learn from a Royalist authority, satisfied with having achieved the victory, left to others (whose motives were less lofty, even as their courage was less sustained) the plunder of those enemies who had yielded to their arms alone. The soldiers unanimously gave God the glory of their great deliverance and victory, and told his lordship, with much cheerfulness, that though they had long fasted and were faint, yet they would willingly want three days longer, rather than give over the service or leave him. Such were the soldiers of Cromwell! And this was no mere talk; for having drained the wells to the mud, they were obliged to drink water out of ditches; and very few of the common soldiers, Mr. Ash assures us, "ate above the quantity of a penny loaf from Tuesday to Saturday morning. That night they kept the field, and the bodies of the dead were stripped."

"In the morning," says the same authority, "there was a mortifying object to behold, when the naked bodies of thousands lay upon the ground, and many not altogether dead." The white smooth skin of numbers gave reason to think that they were gentlemen, and that they might have more honourable burial than the rest, if their friends pleased. Sir Charles Lucas was desired to go along to view the corpses, and choose whom he would, which he did; but would not say he knew any one of them, (not wishing, it would seem, that the great loss the King had sustained should be known,) except one gentleman, who had a bracelet of hair about his wrist. Sir Charles desired the bracelet might be taken off, and said that an honourable lady would give thanks for that. As he passed along, he said, in the presence of many, "Alas, for King Charles! unhappy King Charles!" And indeed the loss of the Monarch was terrible. His northern armies were destroyed, and his power in that quarter paralyzed. The whole of the ammunition and baggage had been taken, and about a hundred colours, and ten thousand arms. Fifteen hundred prisoners fell into the hands of the Parliament ; amongst whom were above a hundred officers, including Sir Charles Lucas, and Major-generals Porter and Tillier. The countrymen (who were commanded to bury the corpses) reported the number slain to be four thousand one hundred and fifty ; and of these, it was calculated that nearly three thousand were of the royal army, and two-thirds of gentle birth.

Among the Royalists of station who fell on this fatal field, were the Lord Eure (who was succeeded in his title by his cousin, a determined supporter of the Parliament's cause) ; the hopeful Lionel, Lord Carey, eldest son of the Earl of Monmouth ; Sir Charles Slingsby, and Colonel John Fenwicke, one of the cavalier members who had deserted from Westminster.* Another name which we find in the list of officers killed on the King's side, is Master Towneley, a Lancashire Papist ; and connected with his death, a family tradition has been handed down, seemingly on good authority, which deserve recital. " Mary, daughter of Sir Francis Trappes, married Charles Towneley, of Towneley in Lanca-shire, Esq., who was killed at the battle of Marston Moor. During the engagement, she was with her father at Knaresboro', where she heard of her husband's fate, and came upon the field the next morning in order to search for his body, while the attendants of the camp were stripping and burying

---

* And many more. It is said that Lord Byron and his three brothers were all killed !

the dead. Here she was accosted by a general officer, to whom she told her melancholy story. He heard her with great tenderness ; but earnestly desired her to leave a place where, besides the distress of witnessing such a scene, she might probably be insulted. She complied ; and he called a trooper, who took her *en-croupe* On her way to Knaresbro', she enquired of the man the name of the officer to whose civility she had been indebted, and learned that it was Lieut-general Cromwell. She survived a widow till 1690, died at Towneley, and was interred in the family chapel at Burnley, aged 91."

It was nearly twelve o'clock the next day before news of the result of the battle reached the Earl of Leven. At length, says the gentleman to whom we are indebted for the account of the Earl's flight, there arrives an express, sent by David Leslie, to acquaint the General they had obtained a most glorious victory, and that the Prince with his broken troops was fled from York. This intelligence was somewhat amazing to those gentlemen that had been eye-witnesses to the disorder of the army before , their retiring, and had accompanied the General in his flight. The Earl himself being much wearied, the evening of the battle, with ordering his army, and now quite spent with his long journey in the night, had cast himself down upon a bed to rest ; when, our informant coming quietly into his chamber, he awoke, and hastely cries out, " Lieutenant-colonel, what news ? "— " All is safe, may it please your Excellence ; the Parliament's army has obtained a great victory ! "

and then he delivers the letter. The General, upon hearing this, knocked upon his breast, and says, " I would to God I had died upon the place ! " and then opens the letter, which in a few lines gave an account of the victory, and in the close pressed his speedy return to the army ; and he accordingly returned the next day.

The news of the Parliament's victory was an unexpected event to others, as well as to the Earl of Leven. Even so late as the morning of the 10th of July, one of Manchester's officers, " passing Hull-ward, for the relief of his wearisomeness," found all the places possessed with the noise of the total overthrow of the Parliament's forces. The first intelligence of the true result of the battle reached Hull on Wednesday, the while the people were assembled in the church to keep a day of humiliation for the success of their army ; and the preacher read to them from the pulpit a letter from Lord Fairfax to the Mayor of Hull, which ran in these words : " Mr. Mayor, after a dark cloud, it hath pleased God to show the sunshine of His glory in victory over his enemies, who are driven into the walls of York, many of their chief officers slain, and all their ordnance and ammunition taken, with small loss (I praise God) on our side. This is all I can now write ; resting your assured, Ferdinando Fairfax."

The letter bore the date of the 2nd of July, (a proof that Lord Fairfax had returned to the engagement the same evening,) and it caused such tears of joy as can scarce be believed. The Mayor immediately transmitted a copy of this letter to the committee of both kingdoms at London, where it arrived on the following Friday. But the Royalists (especially in the prisons) swore it was a forged thing. On Saturday, however, came a letter from the Earl of Manchester (dated from Marston on the 3rd) to a great personage, confirming most of the particulars. But the Royalists still refused to give credence to the news.

Meanwhile, the condition of the wounded received proper notice. Sidney, son of the Earl of Leicester, received many scars. Oliver lost his nephew, Capt. Valentine Walton, whose leg was obliged to be amputated, whereof he died. The poor wounded youth had to lie on the field at Marston while the battle was fought! It was then that Cromwell addressed to Colonel Walton the letter from which I have already made more than one quotation. He speaks thus of his success:—
" Truly England and the Church of GOD hath had a great favor from the Lord, in this great victory, given unto us, such as the like never was since the war began. We never charged but we routed the enemy. The left wing, which I commanded, being composed of our own horse—save a few Scots in our rear—beat all the Prince's horse. GOD made them as stubble to our swords. The particulars I cannot relate now ; but I believe of twenty thousand, the Prince hath not four thousand left. Give glory, all the glory, to GOD ! "

Of course, York surrendered almost immediately afterwards to the Parliament's armies, which then separated again,— Manchester and Cromwell returning to Lincolnshire.

Great disputes arose as to the comparative merits of the several divisions engaged ; and it is to these disputes that many garbled and incorrect versions of the battle exist. The Scots met with a great deal of obloquy for the flight of their centre under Leven. Cromwell's party got the start in the account of the news to London, which was brought by Major Harrison, afterwards the celebrated general of that name. But all accounts of those engaged in the battle agree in praising Cromwell and the Ironsides ; though, of course, in different degrees, according to their several religious and political leanings. Lord Clarendon calls him a " great wicked man ; " and I cannot conclude without noticing that few agreed with him afterwards in the execution of King Charles at Whitehall, 1649. I have spoken of him merely as a Soldier and Cavalry General : and in this character he stands to this day almost unrivalled. I question whether there ever was a greater : and his soldiers were the terror of all Europe till his death, in 1658. Carlyle says he was the greatest Englishman that ever lived.

My chief authorities for the foregoing account of the battle are a " Letter to the Committee of both Kingdoms," signed, July 6, 1644, Leven, Fairfax, Manchester, from the Leaguer before York, inserted in the Journals of the Lords, July 10, 1644.* " The Life of the Marquis of Newcastle by his Wife, 1673." "Diary, &c.," by Sir Henry Slingsby,

* Sanford's Studies and Illustrations of the Great Rebellion.
1858.

who of course knew the ground well. " Fairfax's
Short Memorials," published in the Somer's Tracts.
" Carte's Letters of Ormond." The various Letters
and Accounts of Eye-witnesses in the Newspapers
and among the " King's Papers " in the British
Museum, London. " D'Ewes' Journal," for one
of scout-master, or, in modern terms, Serjeant
Watson's Letters, before quoted. And, finally,
" Carlyle's Letters of Cromwell," and " Warbur-
ton's Rupert and the Cavaliers." Modern accounts
are worthless, though Goldsmith gives a very terse
and correct account of the battle. Guizot, the
French historian of the present day, speaks of the
battle as a mere mêlée ;—in my opinion, a very
unfair description of it. I do not think it worth
translating ; but there are many living Frenchmen
who know better ; among whom I may instance
one, viz., the Emperor Louis Napoleon, with whom
I have often conversed upon it.